DATE DUE

WORLD HERITAGE

Protecting Ecosystems

Brendan and Debbie Gallagher

This edition first published in 2011 in the United States of America by Smart Apple Media. All rights reserved. No part of this book may be reproduced in any form or by any means without written permission from the publisher.

Smart Apple Media
P.O. Box 3263
Mankato, MN, 56002

First published in 2010 by
MACMILLAN EDUCATION AUSTRALIA PTY LTD
15–19 Claremont St, South Yarra, Australia 3141

Visit our web site at www.macmillan.com.au or go directly to www.macmillanlibrary.com.au

Associated companies and representatives throughout the world.

Copyright © Brendan and Debbie Gallagher 2010

Library of Congress Cataloging-in-Publication Data

Gallagher, Brendan.
    Protecting ecosystems : Brendan and Debbie Gallagher.
       p. cm. — (World heritage)
    Includes index.
    ISBN 978-1-59920-579-3 (library bound)
    1. Environmental protection—Juvenile literature. I. Gallagher, Debbie, 1969– II. Title.
    TD170.15.G35 2011
    333.95'16—dc22
                            2009053134

Publisher: Carmel Heron
Managing Editor: Vanessa Lanaway
Editor: Kirstie Innes-Will
Proofreader: Paige Amor
Designer: Kerri Wilson
Page layout: Kerri Wilson
Photo researcher: Legend Images
Illustrator: Guy Holt
Production Controller: Vanessa Johnson

Manufactured in China by Macmillan Production (Asia) Ltd.
Kwun Tong, Kowloon, Hong Kong
Supplier Code: CP December 2009

Acknowledgments

The author and the publisher are grateful to the following for permission to reproduce copyright material:

Cover photograph of soft coral and anthias fish at Pixie Pinnacle, Great Barrier Reef courtesy of Photolibrary/Perrine Doug

Photographs courtesy of:
At A Glance Pty Ltd, 29; © Wayne Lawler; Ecoscene/Corbis, 26; © NASA/Corbis, 6; © Kevin Schafer/Corbis, 23; © Collart Herve/ Corbis Sygma, 8; SambaPhoto/Araquem Alcantara/Getty Images, 9; Kevin Schafer/Getty Images, 21; Walter Meayers Edwards/ National Geographic Stock, 15; Tim Laman/National Geographic Stock, 25; Patricio Robles Gil/Minden Pictures/National Geographic Stock, 14; Photolibrary/Perrine Doug, 1, 10; Photolibrary/Fletcher & Baylis, 13; Photolibrary/Stephen Ingram, 22; Photolibrary/Suzanne Long, 20; Photolibrary/Matthew Scubazoo/SPL, 12; Photolibrary/David Wall, 28; Photolibrary/Allan White, 7; Photolibrary/Konrad Wothe, 16, 17; © NHPA/Photoshot, 24; Plitvice National Park photo by Rita Schlamberger, 19; © Lawrence Cruciana/Shutterstock, 11; © Roman Czupryniak/Shutterstock, 18; © Rusty Dodson/Shutterstock, 30; © Harry H Marsh/Shutterstock, 31; © charles taylor/Shutterstock, 27.

While every care has been taken to trace and acknowledge copyright, the publisher tenders their apologies for any accidental infringement where copyright has proved untraceable. Where the attempt has been unsuccessful, the publisher welcomes information that would redress the situation.

Please note
At the time of printing, the Internet addresses appearing in this book were correct. Owing to the dynamic nature of the Internet, however, we cannot guarantee that all these addresses will remain correct.

Contents

When a word in the text is printed in **bold,** look for its meaning in the glossary boxes.

World Heritage

There are places around the world that are important to all peoples. We call these places the world's heritage. Some of these places are human creations, such as the pyramids of Egypt. Some are natural creations, such as the Great Barrier Reef of Australia.

The World Heritage List

The World Heritage List is a list of **sites** that must be protected because they have some kind of outstanding importance for the world. This list was created in 1972, and new places are added every year. Each site on the World Heritage List belongs to one of the following categories:

 NATURAL – for example, waterfalls, forests, or deserts

 CULTURAL – for example, a building or a site where an event occurred

 MIXED – if it has both natural and cultural features

UNESCO

UNESCO, the United Nations Educational, Scientific, and Cultural Organization, is the organization that maintains the World Heritage List. Find out more at www.unesco.org.

World Heritage Criteria

A place can be **inscribed** on the World Heritage List if it meets at least one of these ten **criteria** and is an outstanding example of it. The criteria are:

 i a masterpiece of human creative genius

 ii a site representing the sharing of human ideas

 iii a site representing a special culture or civilization

 iv a historical building or landscape from a period of history

 v a site representing or important to a traditional culture

 vi a site representing an important event, idea, living tradition, or belief

 vii a very beautiful or unique natural site

 viii a site showing evidence of Earth's history

 ix an important ecosystem

 x an important natural habitat for species protection

KEY TERMS

sites	places
inscribed	added to
criteria	rules or requirements

4

Protecting Ecosystems

Protecting Ecosystems is about protecting communities of plant and animal species that depend on one another. An **ecosystem** contains **habitats** and all the living things within them: animals, birds, insects, trees, plants, etc. An ecosystem also includes non-living parts, such as air, water, rocks, and mountains. These living and non-living things interact with one another to form the ecosystem. Ecosytems are important for **biodiversity**. Biodiversity is an indication of the health of our planet.

Criteria for Protecting Ecosystems

Many of the places in this book are important for many reasons. This book focuses on just one reason: how the places in this book are among the most outstanding ecosystems on Earth. This is reason ix on the list of criteria for being on the World Heritage List.

Protecting World Heritage

Governments around the world have all agreed to protect the sites on the World Heritage List. A site that is not being properly looked after may be put on the List of World Heritage in Danger. See http://whc.unesco.org/en/158/

This map shows the location of the World Heritage sites covered in this book.

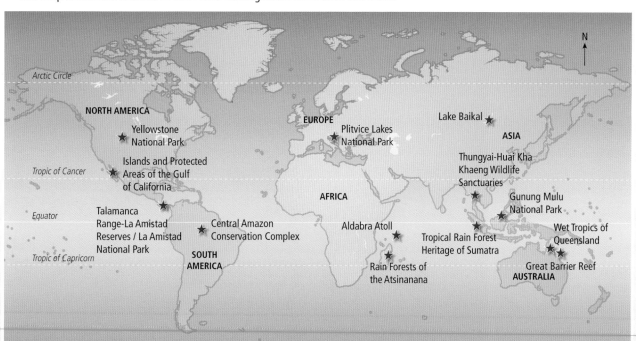

species	groups of plants or animals that have something in common
ecosystem	a community of plants and animals
habitats	places where animals or plants live or grow
biodiversity	the variety of living things in an area

Aldabra Atoll

Aldabra Atoll is a ring-shaped group of islands, which are part of the Seychelles. The four larger islands of the **atoll** surround a **lagoon**. Because Aldabra Atoll is far from other land areas it has its own complete ecosystem. This is made up of many different habitats, including coral reefs, **mangroves**, and **sea grass** meadows. Other small islands form part of the World Heritage area, including Assumption Island, to the south.

FACT FILE

Aldabra Atoll protects coral reef and island ecosystems.

Biodiversity: more than 200 fish species and about 50 coral species

Category:

Criteria:

An ancient volcano lies beneath the Aldabra Atoll ecosystem.

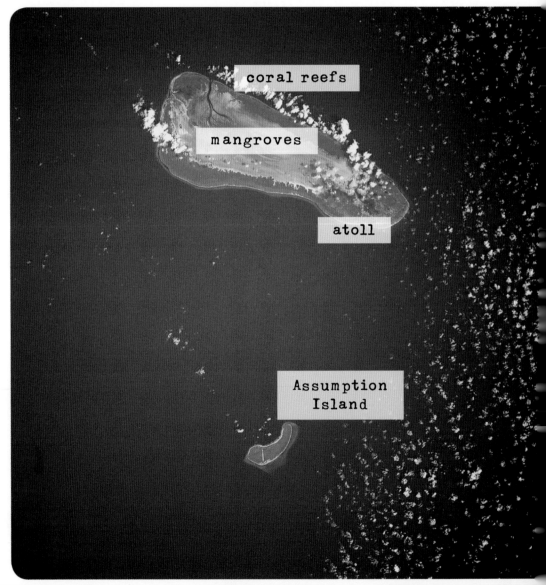

coral reefs

mangroves

atoll

Assumption Island

TIMELINE

125,000 years ago	1967	1976	1982
The Aldabra Atoll forms as the land rises above sea level.	Plans to turn the atoll into a military base are abandoned.	The atoll becomes a protected nature reserve.	Aldabra Atoll is inscribed on the World Heritage List.

The atoll does not rise more than 26 feet (8 meters) above sea level.

Important Features

Aldabra Atoll is the one of Earth's largest atolls. As the coral reef rose above sea level, plants and grasses began to grow on it. This created a habitat for many different species, including giant tortoises and green turtles.

Issues

Global warming is beginning to have an impact on Aldabra Atoll. The atoll is very low. Even slight rises in sea level will **erode** parts of the islands of the atoll and will lead to loss of food sources for the giant tortoises.

Did You Know?

Most coral atolls, including Aldabra, are formed on the circular rims of dead volcanoes that lie below sea level.

GLOSSARY

atoll	a coral island shaped like a ring
lagoon	a body of water cut off from the sea
mangroves	areas of trees growing in salt water
sea grass	grass-like plants that grow in the sea
global warming	increases in temperatures on Earth
erode	wore away

Central Amazon Conservation Complex

The Central Amazon Conservation Complex in Brazil is the largest protected area in the Amazon **rain forest**. Many rivers flow through the area. The ecosystem is very **diverse**.

In the wet season, the rivers flood parts of the Amazon forest, as shown here, but in the dry season this land has white sandy beaches.

rain forest

River Negro flows into the Amazon River

TIMELINE

1960s	1980	2000	2003
Farming and logging begin in the Amazon.	Part of the Central Amazon is protected as a national park.	The site is inscribed on the World Heritage List.	The protected area is more than doubled in size.

Important Features

During the wet season, the rivers flood and create swamps. The animals that are best suited to this ecosystem are animals that live in trees or rivers. Two freshwater mammals, both **endemic to** the region – the Amazon manatee and the pink dolphin – search for food in the flooded areas. The manatee eats grasses and plants it cannot reach when the forest is not flooded.

Did You Know?

The area has 64 electric fish species, the highest number in the world.

Issues

Deforestation of the Amazon rain forest has been a serious issue since the 1960s, but the Central Amazon complex is almost untouched by human activities. It is difficult to get to. There are no roads in, and it is not easily accessed by river.

When the Amazon floods the river dolphins can reach new parts of their ecosystem.

GLOSSARY

rain forest	a forest that receives lots of rainfall
diverse	having a wide variety
endemic to	only found in
deforestation	the cutting down and removal of trees

The Great Barrier Reef

The Great Barrier Reef is a 1,429-mile (2,300-kilometer) stretch of coral reefs off the coast of northeastern Australia. The reefs are formed along 600 islands and 300 cays – small, low islands made of coral and sand. The Great Barrier Reef is the largest World Heritage site.

The Great Barrier Reef is the largest protected ecosystem on Earth.

fish

coral

TIMELINE

500,000 years ago	1937	1979	1981
The Great Barrier Reef begins to form.	Two islands of the Great Barrier Reef are made national parks.	Part of the Great Barrier Reef is made a national park.	The Great Barrier Reef is inscribed on the World Heritage List.

Important Features

More than 2,900 different reefs form the Great Barrier Reef. They have been created by millions of tiny sea animals called hard corals. The reefs attract thousands of different sea creatures. Many of these sea creatures feed on one another.

Loggerhead turtles eat thousands of jellyfish in the Great Barrier Reef, helping to maintain the ecosystem.

Issues

The greatest threat to the Great Barrier Reef is **global warming**. Increases in the Earth's temperature are in turn increasing ocean temperatures. This can damage or even kill coral. Without the coral there can be no Great Barrier Reef ecosystem.

GLOSSARY

sea grass	grass-like plants that grow in the sea
mangroves	areas of trees growing in salt water
global warming	increases in temperatures on Earth

Gunung Mulu National Park

Gunung Mulu National Park is a **rain forest** on the island of Borneo, Malaysia. There are many mountains in the park, formed from a rock called limestone. Caves form easily in limestone, and one of the park's mountains, Gunung Api, has more caves than any other mountain in the world.

The caves of Gunung Mulu form unique ecosystems. Many of the animal species living there never leave them.

FACT FILE

MALAYSIA ★
Borneo

Gunung Mulu protects mountain rain forest, **lowland rain forest**, and cave ecosystems.

Biodiversity: 3,500 plant species, 80 mammal species, and 270 bird species, of which 24 species are **endemic to** Borneo

Category:

Criteria:

Gunung Api

Deer Cave

lowland rain forest

TIMELINE

5 million years ago	1974	1985	2000
The oldest of Gunung Mulu's caves begins to form.	The area is named a national park.	Gunung Mulu National Park is opened to the public.	The site is inscribed on the World Heritage List.

Gunung Mulu National Park contains the largest known cave chamber in the world.

Important Features

Millions of bats and birds called *swiftlets* live in the caves of Gunung Mulu. They feed on insects. Other species that live in the caves rely on the bats and swiftlets. Snakes, rats, and monitor lizards eat fallen birds and bats, and insects feed on their dung and droppings. Then spiders, scorpions, and cave geckos feed on the insects.

Did You Know?

The park is best known for its 27 bat species. In Deer Cave at Gunung Api, there are 3 million bats.

Issues

One of the most serious issues facing the park is **deforestation** outside the park boundaries. Bats and cave swiftlets will feed up to 15.5 miles (25 kilometers) from their caves. It is important not to cut down trees within that distance.

GLOSSARY

rain forest	a forest that receives a lot of rainfall
lowland rain forest	a rain forest that is not high above sea level
endemic to	only found in
deforestation	the cutting down and removal of trees

Islands and Protected Areas of the Gulf of California

The Islands and Protected Areas of the Gulf of California is a collection of nine protected areas in the west of Mexico. The ecosystem is very **diverse**.

The Gulf of California site includes 244 desert and rocky islands, as well as the marine ecosystem.

FACT FILE

The Gulf of California protects island, coastal, and **marine** ecosystems.

Biodiversity: more than 695 plant species, 31 species of **cetaceans**, and 900 fish species, of which 90 are **endemic to** the area

Category:

Criteria:

mainland coast

island

desert

Espiritu Santo Island

Gulf of California

TIMELINE

4.5 million years ago
The Cortez Sea is created as the Baja California Peninsula breaks away from the mainland.

2005
The site is inscribed on the World Heritage List.

2007
The Islas Marietas National Park is added to the listing for the Islands and Protected Areas of the Gulf of California.

Important Features

About one third of the world's cetaceans can be found in the Gulf of California, including five of the world's eight sea turtles. One of the cetaceans, the rare vaquita porpoise, is endemic to the area. Vaquitas feed on small fish and squid not more than 15.5 miles (25 kilometers) from the shore.

These short-beaked dolphins are some of the many cetaceans found in the Gulf of California.

Issues

In 2008, the Mexican government canceled over 1,000 fishing permits to protect the World Heritage site. They were particularly worried about the natural habitat of the vaquita porpoise, the smallest cetacean in the world. However, plans to build harbors and docks for yachts along the coast of the Sea of Cortez could also affect the marine ecosystem.

GLOSSARY

diverse	having a wide variety
marine	of the ocean
cetaceans	mammals that live in the sea
endemic to	only found in

Lake Baikal

Lake Baikal, in the center of the Russian Federation, is the oldest and deepest lake in the world. It is surrounded by **deciduous forests** and forests of **conifers**.

FACT FILE

RUSSIAN FEDERATION

Lake Baikal protects the best example of a freshwater ecosystem on Earth.

Biodiversity: 1,900 species of plants and animals, almost one half of which are **endemic to** the area

Category:

Criteria:

About 1,200 animal species live in the waters of Lake Baikal.

mountain ranges

coniferous forests

Lake Baikal

TIMELINE

5 million years ago	1916	1957	1996
Lake Baikal begins to form.	Part of the northeast coast of Lake Baikal is made a nature reserve.	A paper mill is built on the shores of Lake Baikal.	Lake Baikal is inscribed on the World Heritage List.

Important Features

There are more golomyanka fish in Lake Baikal than any other species of fish. The golomyanka is eaten by the only freshwater seal in the world, the Baikal seal. Baikal seals eat about 41 million golomyanka per day, preventing the golomyanka from eating too many other fish in the lake and changing the ecosystem.

Did You Know?
Lake Baikal is 5,374 feet (1,638 meters) deep and contains 20 percent of the world's unfrozen freshwater.

Issues

The paper mill built at Lake Baikal has polluted a large area of the lake. It produces some of the worst air pollution in Russia. The mill needs to be closed, but 3,500 people work there and closing it would ruin the local town. A solution could be to change the mill to perform a different type of work that has less impact on the ecosystem.

The Baikal seals eat enough golomyanka fish to keep the Lake Baikal ecosystem in balance.

GLOSSARY

deciduous forests	forests of trees that lose their leaves once a year
conifers	trees or shrubs like pine trees that grow seeds on cones
endemic to	only found in

Plitvice Lakes National Park

Plitvice Lakes National Park in Croatia is a forested area with 16 lakes and three main rivers. The main species of tree is beech, which makes up about three-quarters of the forests. Plitvice is one of the last remaining examples of the **temperate forest** ecosystem that once covered the continent of Europe.

lakes

beech forest

waterfalls

TIMELINE

About 7,000 years ago
Much of Europe was covered in temperate forests.

1928
The area is made a national park.

1979
The site is inscribed on the World Heritage List.

1991
The Croatian War of Independence begins and Serbian forces take over Plitvice.

1992
The site is placed on the List of World Heritage in Danger.

1995
The Croatian War of Independence ends.

1997
The area is removed from the List of World Heritage in Danger.

Important Features

Plitvice protects many mammal species. Wild boars live in the forests, digging in the ground for mushrooms, insects, and whatever else they can find. Deer roam the park, eating leaves, bark, and fruits. Brown bears – once common throughout Europe, but now very rare – also live in the forests.

Many mammals, including bears, are found in Plitvice. They once lived throughout Europe but are now rare.

Issues

In 1992, the park was placed on the List of World Heritage in Danger because Croatia was at war with its neighbor, Serbia. Serbian forces took over Plitvice and there were no park managers. Bears were hunted, and dynamite was used for fishing. Since the war ended, park managers have repaired the damage done to the park.

GLOSSARY

temperate forest   a forest in an area with a mild climate

Rain Forests of the Atsinanana

Rain Forests of the Atsinanana is a group of six **rain forests** along the east of the island of Madagascar. These **diverse** forests make up less than 10 percent of the forest that once covered the area.

The Rain Forests of the Atsinanana have some of the world's most diverse habitats.

mountains

cliffs

rain forest

TIMELINE

60 million years ago	2,000 years ago	1927	1997–99	2007
Madagascar becomes an island.	The first people arrive on the island of Madagascar.	Twelve natural reserves are created on the island.	The six areas of Atsinanana are made national parks.	The site is inscribed on the World Heritage List.

Important Features

Because humans did not live on Madagascar for a long time, many unique species developed there without human interference. Up to 99 different species of lemurs, a type of **primate**, are endemic to Madagascar. While looking for food, some lemurs take pollen from one plant to another, which enables more plants to grow. The fossa, a ferret-like **carnivore** found in the Rain Forests of the Atsinanana, preys on lemurs.

Issues

Many of the people living around the site are poor. They view the rain forests as places where they can get food, or as land they can clear to plant crops. The local people need to be educated and given support in finding other ways to get food.

Lemurs play an important role in the ecosystem by spreading pollen.

Did You Know?

Madagascar's Madame Berthe's mouse lemur is the smallest primate in the world, weighing 1 ounce (30 grams).

GLOSSARY

rain forests	forests that receive a lot of rainfall
diverse	having a wide variety
endemic to	only found in
primate	a member of the group of mammals that includes monkeys, apes, and humans
carnivore	an animal that eats meat

Talamanca Range-
La Amistad Reserves/
La Amistad National Park

FACT FILE

COSTA RICA
PANAMA   SOUTH
AMERICA

La Amistad protects a unique rain forest ecosystem.

Biodiversity: 215 mammal species, of which 13 are **endemic to** the World Heritage area; more than 1,000 species of flowering plants

Category:

Criteria:

La Amistad is a land bridge, connecting species from North and South America.

Talamanca Range-La Amistad Reserves / La Amistad National Park is a single **rain forest**. Because the area is split between two different countries, Costa Rica and Panama, it has two different names. The two countries agreed to combine La Amistad as one World Heritage site in 1990. La Amistad is unique because it is the point where the animal and plant species from North and South America meet one another.

mountains

rain forest

TIMELINE

25,000 years ago	1964	1983	1990
The La Amistad area is forested.	Part of the area is protected as a forest reserve.	Talamanca Range-La Amistad Reserves, Costa Rica, is inscribed on the World Heritage List.	La Amistad National Park, Panama, is added to the World Heritage List.

Important Features

La Amistad is the largest natural forest in Central America. It is one of the last places where all of the large cats of Central America still exist, including ocelots, jaguars, and pumas. These **carnivores** feed on birds, reptiles, and small mammals in the forest.

Issues

The park is being poorly managed, with forest being cleared for farming and other destructive uses. A **hydro-electric** dam is planned on the south side of the park in Costa Rica. La Amistad may one day be placed on the List of World Heritage in Danger.

Did You Know?

La Amistad forest is partly protected from development because the lands of seven **indigenous peoples** surround part of the park.

The ocelot is one of many carnivores in La Amistad.

GLOSSARY

rain forest	a forest that receives a lot of rainfall
endemic to	only found in
carnivores	animals that eat meat
hydro-electric	uses water to produce electricity
deforestation	the cutting down and removal of trees
indigenous peoples	the first peoples to live in an area

Thungyai-Huai Kha Khaeng Wildlife Sanctuaries

Thungyai-Huai Kha Khaeng Wildlife Sanctuaries is a unique **tropical** ecosystem of mountains and valleys in Thailand. The area is made up of two **sanctuaries** that are combined as one World Heritage site that contains nearly all of the forest habitats of South-East Asia, including **deciduous forests**, bamboo forests, and tropical **rain forests**.

FACT FILE

THAILAND

Thungyai-Huai Kha Khaeng protects tropical rain forest, deciduous forest, and freshwater ecosystems.

Biodiversity: 120 mammal species, 400 bird species, 96 reptiles, 43 amphibians, and 113 freshwater fish

Category:

Criteria:

The sanctuaries include 18 mountains that are more than 3,280 feet (1,000 meters) tall. They provide many habitats for animal and plant species.

mountains

valleys

tropical forest

TIMELINE

1972
Huai Kha Khaeng is made an animal sanctuary.

1974
Thungyai is made an animal sanctuary.

1991
The two sanctuaries are joined together and the site is inscribed on the World Heritage List.

Important Features

About three-quarters of Southeast Asia's large mammals can be found in the sanctuaries. Clouded leopards are protected in the sanctuaries, where they prey on smaller mammals, including macaques (a kind of monkey), hog deer, porcupines, and squirrels. These smaller animals feed on insects, fruits, and plants.

Issues

One of the threats facing the sanctuaries comes from **poachers**. Poachers capture animals to sell live, or kill animals to sell their body parts. Sanctuary managers patrol the area to prevent poachers from entering. They also check food sold in local restaurants to make sure that illegally captured animals are not on the menu.

Did You Know?
The sanctuaries have 22 species of woodpecker, more than any other place on Earth.

This hornbill is one of many rare birds in the sanctuaries.

GLOSSARY

tropical	from the hot and humid area between the Tropic of Cancer and the Tropic of Capricorn
sanctuaries	protected parks for animals and plants
deciduous forests	forests of trees that lose their leaves once a year
rain forests	forests that receive a lot of rainfall
poachers	people who hunt animals in an area where it is not allowed

Tropical Rain Forest Heritage of Sumatra

The **Tropical** Rain Forest Heritage of Sumatra is made up of three different areas of **rain forest** on the Indonesian island of Sumatra. It is a volcanic landscape running from the coast to the mountains. It is very **diverse** due to its extreme ranges in **altitude.**

FACT FILE

Sumatra INDONESIA

The Tropical Rain Forest Heritage of Sumatra protects a rain forest ecosystem.

Biodiversity: more than 10,000 species of plants and animals

Category:

Criteria:

The rain forest of Sumatra is under pressure from the people who want more room for farming.

mountains

rain forest

farmland

TIMELINE

1980	1982	1992	2004	2007
Gunung Leuser is made a national park.	Bukit Barisan Selatan is made a national park.	Kerinci Seblat is made a national park.	The three areas are inscribed on the World Heritage List.	The site is considered for the List of World Heritage in Danger because of illegal logging.

Tigers will prey on orangutans, but orangutans stay high in the trees of the forest to keep themselves safe.

Important Features

The vegetation in the mountains of Sumatra is different to the vegetation along the coast. Different animals have adapted to each of these habitats. There are 201 mammal species, including tigers, rhinoceros, elephants, and orangutans, in the area.

Issues

The site is seriously threatened by illegal logging, **deforestation** of the land for farming, **poaching**, and road-building. A single road built into an ecosystem will prevent many animals from moving around freely.

Did You Know?

Orangutans from Sumatra are known to use sticks to catch ants and to hold leaves over their heads when it is raining.

GLOSSARY

tropical	from the hot and humid area between the Tropic of Cancer and the Tropic of Capricorn
rain forest	a forest that receives a lot of rainfall
diverse	having a wide variety
altitude	the height above sea level
deforestation	the cutting down and removal of trees
poaching	hunting or fishing where it is not allowed

Wet Tropics of Queensland

The Wet Tropics of Queensland stretch for about 280 miles (450 kilometers) along the northeast coast of Australia. The area includes coastal and mountainous areas.

FACT FILE

AUSTRALIA

The Wet Tropics of Queensland protects ecosystems of **tropical** forests, **mangroves**, and coral reefs.

Biodiversity:
41 **marsupial** species, 2,845 plant species, and Australia's richest bird community of 314 species

Category:

Criteria:

The Wet Tropics of Queensland includes 19 national parks, including the Daintree National Park.

mountains

Daintree rain forest

beach

ocean

TIMELINE

50 million years ago	1966	1988
Rain forests cover the area on the landmass of **Gondwana**.	A national park is formed to protect the area from logging.	The site is inscribed on the World Heritage List.

Important Features

The rain forests of the Wet Tropics of Queensland are the remains of forests that first grew when Australia was part of the landmass known as Gondwana. Cassowaries, ancient flightless birds, still live in the area. They eat different fruits and spread the seeds around the rain forest through their droppings, giving the plants a chance to grow again.

Issues

There are many threats to this ecosystem. Roads, electricity lines, and dams were built in the area before it became a World Heritage site. They break up natural habitats. Managers of the area have built rope bridges and underpasses over and above roads so animals can move around safely. Power lines are raised up very high to allow the rain forest to grow to its natural height.

Rope bridges enable animals such as possums to move safely to different areas within the Wet Tropics of Queensland.

Did You Know?
There are 58 species of frog living in the Wet Tropics of Queensland.

GLOSSARY

tropical	from the hot and humid area between the Tropic of Cancer and the Tropic of Capricorn
mangroves	areas of trees growing in salt water
marsupial	a kind of mammal that carries its young in a pouch
Gondwana	the large, ancient continent which was made up of what are now Africa, South America, Antarctica, and Australia

Yellowstone National Park

Yellowstone National Park is a forested area in the Rocky Mountains. The park is about 6,562 feet (2,000 meters) above sea level, surrounded by mountains rising 13,123 feet (4,000 meters). **Conifers** grow easily at this **altitude**. Yellowstone is at the center of the largest ecosystem in the mainland part of the United States.

FACT FILE

UNITED STATES

Yellowstone National Park protects forest ecosystems.

Biodiversity: 67 mammal species, including mountain lions, wolves, bears, and bison

Category:

Criteria:

Rocky Mountains

lodgepole pines

Yellowstone Lake

Yellowstone Lake is one of the largest lakes in North America.

TIMELINE

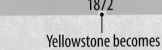

1872
Yellowstone becomes the world's first national park.

1978
Yellowstone is inscribed on the World Heritage List.

1995
Yellowstone is placed on the List of World Heritage in Danger.

2003
Yellowstone is removed from the List of World Heritage in Danger.

Important Features

About 80 percent of Yellowstone National Park is covered in forests of lodgepole pines. Intense heat from fire is needed to release the seeds inside the pine cones. Fires are a natural part of Yellowstone's ecosystem. More than 90 percent of the fires in the park are allowed to burn.

Issues

A fish called the cutthroat trout, which lives in Yellowstone Lake, is under threat from **introduced species**. This is one of the reasons why Yellowstone was placed on the List of World Heritage in Danger in 1995. Each introduced trout can eat up to 40 cutthroat trout a year. Park managers are trying to remove the introduced trout to protect the natural ecosystem.

Did You Know?
Yellowstone National Park is a volcanic area that experiences about 1,000 earthquakes each year.

Native species, such as bald eagles, feed on the cutthroat trout but do not eat enough to upset the ecosystem.

GLOSSARY

conifers	trees or shrubs like pine trees that grow seeds on cones
altitude	the height above sea level
introduced species	plants or animals that are not native to an area

Index